Living in Harsh Lands

By Richard Lawrence

EDUCATION RESOURCE SERVICE

GLASGOW

Series Literacy Consultant
Dr Ros Fisher

PEARSON
Longman

Pearson Education Limited
Edinburgh Gate
Harlow
Essex CM20 2JE
England

www.longman.co.uk

DK

The following people from **DK** have
contributed to the development of this product:

Art Director Rachael Foster

Martin Wilson **Managing Art Editor**	**Managing Editor** Marie Greenwood
Polly Appleton **Design**	**Editorial** Selina Wood
Brenda Clynch **Picture Research**	**Production** Gordana Simakovic
Richard Czapnik, Andy Smith **Cover Design**	**DTP** David McDonald

Consultant David Green

Dorling Kindersley would like to thank: Rose Horridge, Hayley Smith and Gemma Woodward in the DK Picture Library;
Simon Mumford for cartography; Penny Smith for editorial assistance; Johnny Pau for additional cover design work.

Contents

Introduction

Some people live in the hottest, coldest, wettest and driest parts of the planet. People of different **cultures**, or ways of life, learn to adapt to the harsh or extreme climates in which they live. A group's culture includes all of its beliefs, customs and traditions. Types of food, dwellings, tools and occupations are also part of a culture.

This book will introduce you to a variety of cultures, from those of the tropical rainforest to those of the frozen Arctic tundra. You can learn how people have adapted to such extreme environments by making the best use of the resources around them. You can also discover how they have adjusted to life in the modern world while keeping their culture.

The Bedouins thrive in the extremely hot, dry climate of the desert.

Life in Hot, Dry Lands

About one-third of the Earth's land is hot and dry. This land includes **deserts**, **semi-deserts** and **savannahs**. These lands present challenges to all forms of life.

Deserts are the driest places on Earth with less than 25 centimetres of rain a year. Desert animals and plants have adapted to dry conditions. Camels, scorpions and sand vipers conserve water and avoid the heat of the day. Desert plants, such as cacti, hold water in their stems or roots.

hot, dry lands

Map showing the major hot semi-deserts, deserts and savannahs of the world

Semi-deserts, like those found in Australia, have about 35 centimetres of rainfall a year. Semi-deserts support a little more vegetation than deserts. These plants make it possible for people living there to raise sheep and goats.

Savannahs receive between 5 and 75 centimetres of rain a year. These areas are ideal for grazing animals.

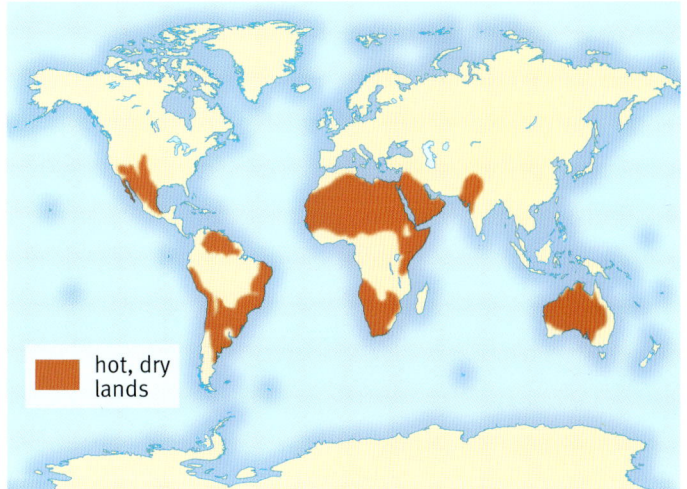

The Negev desert, Israel

The Masai

Many Masai (mah-SY) live on the hot **savannahs** of Kenya and Tanzania, in East Africa. The Masai are often thought of as warriors, but are in fact mainly cow herders.

There are limited resources on the savannah, so the Masai use every part of the cows they herd. The milk is drunk every day. Cattle are also used as a source of meat. Their hides are used for clothing. Even their dung is used to construct buildings and provide fuel for fires. Because of their usefulness cattle are given as gifts for births, initiations and marriages.

The Masai were **nomads**. They herded their cattle across the Great Rift Valley. They migrated to avoid over-grazing or to search for a better water supply. Because their dwellings were easy to build, they simply abandoned them, and moved to a better place.

Map showing where the Masai people live

Masai herding cattle in Kenya

In the 1800s, Europeans took over Masai land for farms, ranches and parks. The Masai fought for their land but eventually lost two-thirds of their territory. Many were squeezed into the least fertile areas. Without the land and resources to raise cattle, the Masai found it even more difficult to survive the harsh climate. Despite efforts to convince them to settle, most Masai are still nomadic.

The Masai have been unwilling to abandon their traditional **culture**. The loss of land has brought extreme poverty. As a result, some Masai have moved to cities.

The Masai who work in businesses and government maintain some of their traditional culture. Some Masai now own camps and guest ranches on the savannahs. They welcome tourists to join them on safaris. Money from these businesses helps the Masai maintain their land and traditions.

Beaded necklaces are part of the traditional Masai dress.

The permanent home of a Masai family is made from wooden poles covered with dry cow dung, with a grass roof.

Rite of Passage

To become a man, a Masai youth traditionally had to kill a lion single-handedly with a spear. The government of Kenya has outlawed this practice.

The Bedouins

The Bedouins (BED-oo-ihns) are Arabic-speaking **nomads** who live in the **deserts** of the Middle East and northern Africa. These desert climates present the Bedouins with the challenges of extreme heat and cold, little water, sandstorms and sun glare. Bedouins have adapted to the harsh climates by travelling with herds of camels, horses, sheep and goats in search of grass and water.

For shelter, the Bedouins weave tents of goat hair. The goat hair reflects the warmth of the sun while keeping the inside of the tent cool. When the weather is cold or wet, the goat hair acts as insulation, keeping in the warmth of a fire. The tents are simple to put up and take down and are easy to carry.

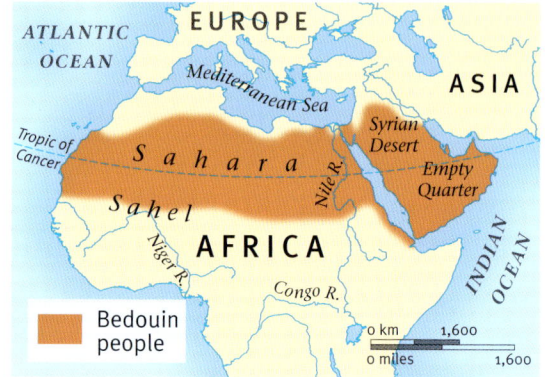

Map showing the deserts where the Bedouin people live

Looping sheep's wool onto a spindle

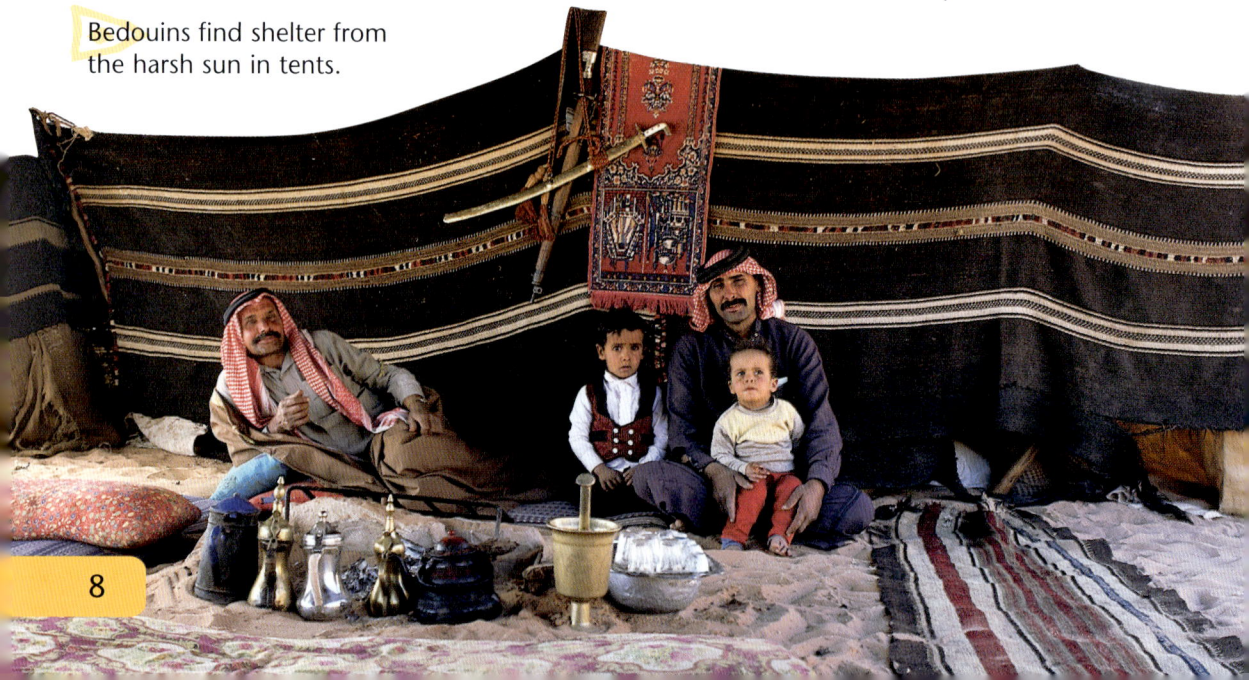

Bedouins find shelter from the harsh sun in tents.

Bedouins make their clothing to suit the climate. The traditional Bedouin men wear a long, white tunic and a head cloth in the hottest months. These clothes reflect the bright sunlight and protect against blowing sand. Bedouin women are known for their spinning and weaving. They use the hair from their animals to produce colourfully dyed tent cloths, cushion covers, curtains and rugs.

Many Bedouin children wear modern clothes.

Many Bedouins have given up their traditional lifestyle, and have settled in towns and cities. Some live in apartments and work in the oil industry. Some Bedouin men wear jackets and trousers rather than traditional tunic and head cloth.

However, many of the 5 million Bedouins in the Middle East still live a partially nomadic life. A family that spends most of the year in a city house may live in a tent for the summer. Some Bedouins also use their traditional skills in new ways. Bedouin men, who are highly skilled trekkers and climbers, often serve as guides and park rangers. Many Bedouin women earn money by selling traditional hand-woven goods in city markets. Used to adapting to the harsh climate of the desert, the Bedouins have proved they can also adapt to living in cities.

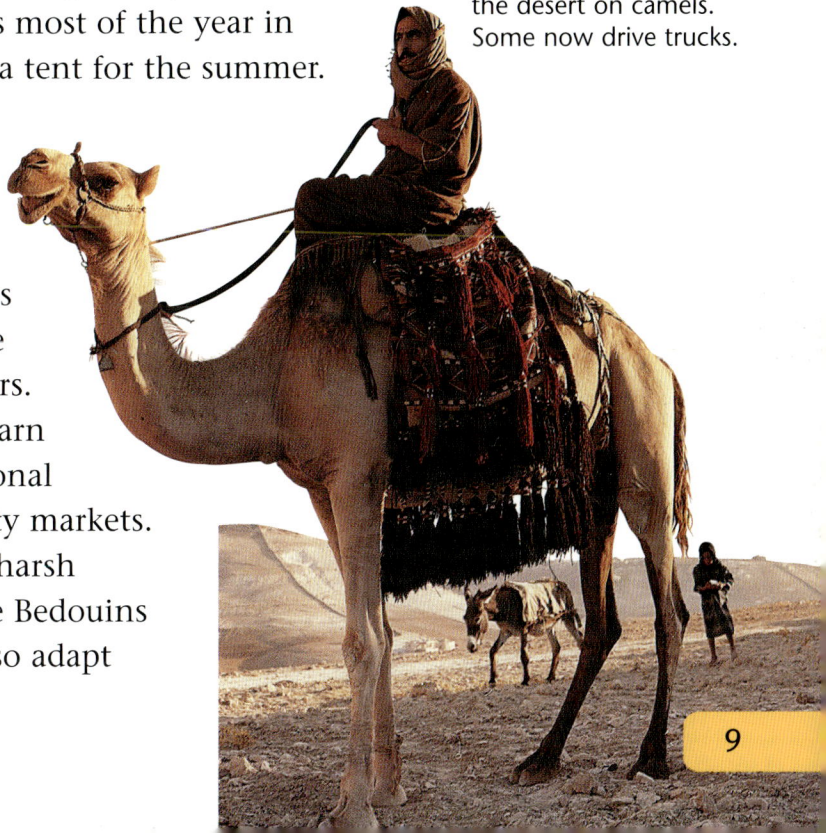
Traditionally, Bedouins have travelled through the desert on camels. Some now drive trucks.

Aboriginal Australians

Originally, the **indigenous** people of Australia lived in about 500 different groups. Each had its own language and traditions. At first, most lived along the coast, but gradually, some of the people spread into the **desert** regions of Australia called the outback.

The Aboriginal people, who make up 2 per cent of the population, live in these regions.

The Aboriginal people were hunters and gatherers. They invented the boomerang, a clever hunting weapon. If it did not hit its target, it circled around and returned to the thrower. That saved energy in the hot, dry outback.

The Aboriginal people moved from place to place to find food and water. Snakes, witchetty grubs and small mammals such as bandicoots were part of their diet. Women ground up grass seeds between stones to make small flat cakes. The Aboriginal people learned how to locate water in deep, hidden springs and to dig up sweet roots to quench their thirst.

Boomerangs were originally used as a hunting weapon.

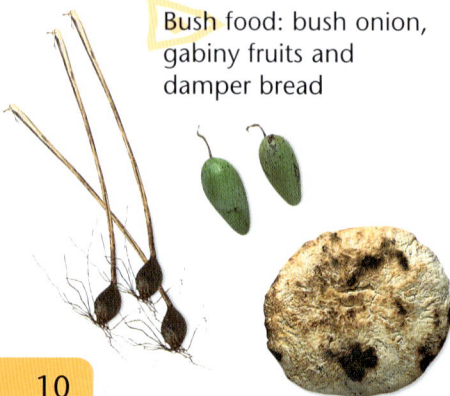

Bush food: bush onion, gabiny fruits and damper bread

Aboriginal dancers

Around campfires, Aboriginal people told stories of the Dreamtime, a time when their ancestor spirits created the world. For thousands of years, the Aboriginal people have made paintings of the Dreamtime on rocks and have drawn patterns in the sand to trace their ancestors' journeys. For many Aboriginal people today, the Dreamtime is an important belief.

Today, most of Australia's 250,000 Aboriginal people live in cities and towns. For many years, the Aboriginal people were denied basic rights. In the 1960s, new laws helped them to gain the right to vote and to receive better housing, jobs and education. They still struggle to regain land taken from them during early European settlement.

Rock art painting of the Lightning Brothers, spirits from the Dreamtime

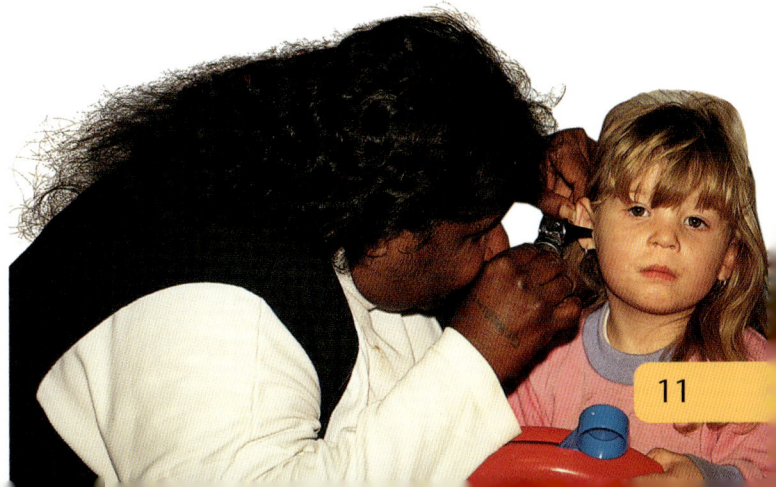

Aboriginal doctor with patient

Life in Cold Lands

Antarctica, a continent equal in size to Europe and the United States combined lies in the far south of the Southern Hemisphere. The temperature of Antarctica never rises above freezing, 0 degrees Celsius. About 98 per cent of the land is covered by ice.

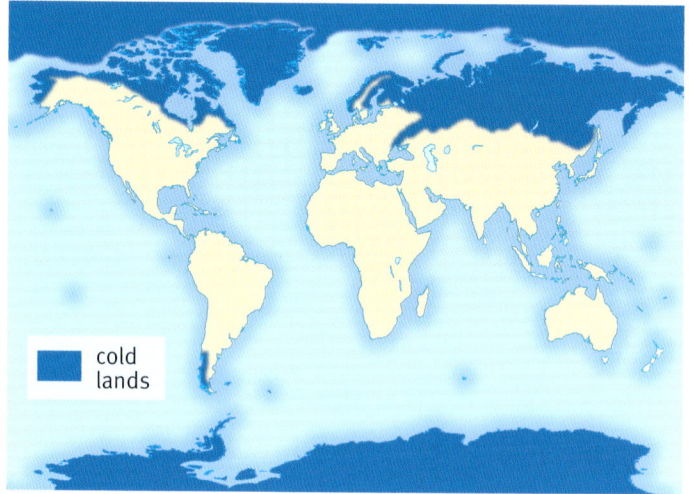

cold lands

Map showing the cold lands of the world

The climate of this continent supports many plants and animals. Lichens, algae and mosses grow in low-lying clusters. By staying close together and near the ground, the plants can trap moisture, block wind and avoid being crushed by the snow.

Although some plants can survive the cold climate, there is not enough vegetation to support land mammals. The coast, however, is home to seals and walruses. There are lots of birds, too. The flightless penguin is Antarctica's best-known bird.

Mosses and lichens can survive in extremely low temperatures.

Penguins on an iceberg in the Weddell Sea, Antarctica

The tundra landscape of north-west Canada

In the far north of the Northern Hemisphere, the Arctic Ocean is a sea of packed ice and icebergs. Arctic lands include parts of Canada, Alaska, the Russian Federation, Greenland, Iceland, Sweden and Norway. Although the temperature can rise as high as 10 degrees Celsius, much of this region is frozen year-round. The polar bear is the only land mammal that travels over the Arctic ice. It hunts the seals that live in the icy ocean.

Tundra is the treeless land surrounding the Arctic Ocean at the northern edges of Europe, Asia and North America. Tundra soil is frozen as far as 50 centimetres below the surface. This frozen soil is called **permafrost**. When the surface thaws in summer, grasses and flowers briefly bloom.

Migratory birds feed and breed on the tundra each summer. Land mammals, including the Arctic fox and wolf, live on the tundra. Their thick coats and sheltered dens help them survive the polar winters. Large animals, such as moose, musk oxen and reindeer (also known as caribou) graze there.

Arctic wolves hunt in packs and mostly eat reindeer.

The Saami

The Saami (SAH-mee) are an **indigenous** people of far northern Europe. Originally, the Saami were hunters, fishers and gatherers. They survived in the cold, harsh climates by using the resources they found there. Fish were plentiful on the coast, and abundant beaver and wild reindeer were hunted on land. In the sixteenth and seventeenth centuries, Saami **culture** changed. Instead of simply hunting the reindeer, the Saami began trapping and taming them to increase their herds. Because their herds grew so large, the Saami had to move from place to place to find good grazing lands. Reindeer became extremely valuable. They were used for pulling sleds as well as for their hides, meat and milk. The Saami language has more than twenty different words for reindeer, showing just how important the animal is to this culture.

Map showing where the Saami people live

Polar Night

In the far north, the sun stays below the horizon for months. This is called *kaamos*, or "polar night". In some places polar night lasts as long as six months, followed by six months of continuous daylight, or "polar day".

This Saami boy is wearing boots made from reindeer fur.

Over the centuries, Saami lands became divided among Norway, Sweden, Finland and Russia. This prevented the Saami from moving along traditional herding routes. As a result, the Saami gradually became more settled.

Like many Saami homes, this house contains a sauna.

Fewer than 75,000 Saami live in Europe's northern-most regions today. Saami families now live in one place and herd their animals to new pastures each autumn, using snowmobiles or helicopters. Schools, newspapers, magazines and a radio station keep Saami language and culture alive. Some traditions are still practised. For example, when their first teeth appear, many Saami children are given their first reindeer. Today, about 40 per cent of Saami live by herding, hunting and fishing – traditional livelihoods. Tourism provides income for many. Others sell *duoji* – crafts such as bonework, antlerwork and lace.

Saami women weaving cloth on a loom

The Inuit and the Yu'pik

The Inuit (IHN-oo-it) of Canada and Greenland and the Yu'pik Eskimo of southern Alaska were **nomads** who hunted sea mammals, reindeer and fish. These animals provided food, materials for shelter, fuel, tools, weapons and clothing.

Map showing where the Inuit and Yu'pik peoples live

In winter, the Inuit and the Yu'pik travelled over the snow on dogsleds to hunt and to ice fish. They built igloos – round snow houses – as temporary shelters. Permanent shelters were made of whalebone, wood, earth and stone. In summer, these native peoples of the North lived in animal-skin tents.

Whatever the Inuit and the Yu'pik needed, they made themselves. Their traditional kayaks, harpoons and fur clothing were hard wearing. To save scarce fuel, they often ate fish and meat raw. Eating raw meat also provided them with nutrients that cooking destroys.

Sled dogs are still used for racing and sometimes for work.

Today many Inuit and Yu'pik live in towns, where their wooden houses are built on stilts above the snow. This helps to keep their homes warm. At school, children learn their native languages as well as their local languages. Many adults keep alive the traditional art of bone and stone carving. These sculptures are popular in art galleries and shops around the world.

They continue to hunt and fish. However, they are more likely to use snowmobiles and vehicles with outboard motors than dogsleds and kayaks. They still enjoy eating reindeer, moose and duck, but they might flavour them with a little ketchup or mustard. *Agutak*, a traditional iced dessert made with oils, berries, sugar and water, is still a popular treat.

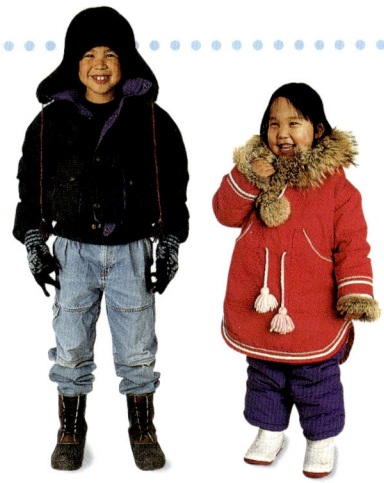

Inuit and Yu'pik children dressed for winter

This soapstone carving is an example of traditional Inuit craft.

The iced dessert known as *agutak*

Arctic peoples use snowmobiles for activities ranging from hunting to shopping.

Life in Wet Lands

Wet lands, such as rainforests and **swamps**, are the opposite of **deserts** in many ways. They have high rainfall and moist soil and abundant plant and animal life.

Tropical rainforests lie near the equator. The Amazon region, in South America, is one of the world's largest rainforests. Rainforests are wet and warm all year-round. At least half the world's plant and animal species live in rainforests.

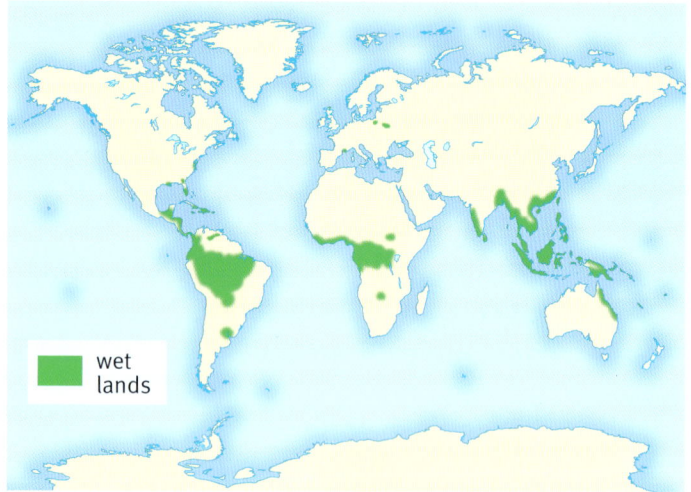

Map showing the rainforests and swamps of the world

The canopy, or top layer, of the Amazon rainforest is thick with leaves and fruit. Monkeys, squirrels, fruit bats and toucans live in the canopy. Eagles fly through, looking for prey. Snakes crawl on tree trunks and branches. Small wild cats, such as clouded leopards hunt in the trees. Big cats, such as jaguars and tigers, prowl the rainforest floor.

The Amazon rainforest covers a vast area—over a billion hectares.

Swamps are lowlands covered with slow-moving water. They are found in temperate, or mild, climates and in tropical ones. The Everglades is a swamp that covers about 7,100 square kilometres in southern Florida, in the United States.

The Florida Everglades is home to alligators, snakes and birds.

The vegetation in a swamp provides nesting and feeding grounds for water birds, such as ducks and herons. Mammals as small as the beaver and as large as the hippopotamus live in swamps, as do reptiles, amphibians and fish.

A **flood plain** is the flat land along a river that floods periodically when the river level rises. Floods deposit sediment, making the plain fertile.

Rice grows well in the flood plains at Guilin, China.

Hippopotamuses live in the rivers and swamps of Africa, taking refuge from the hot sun.

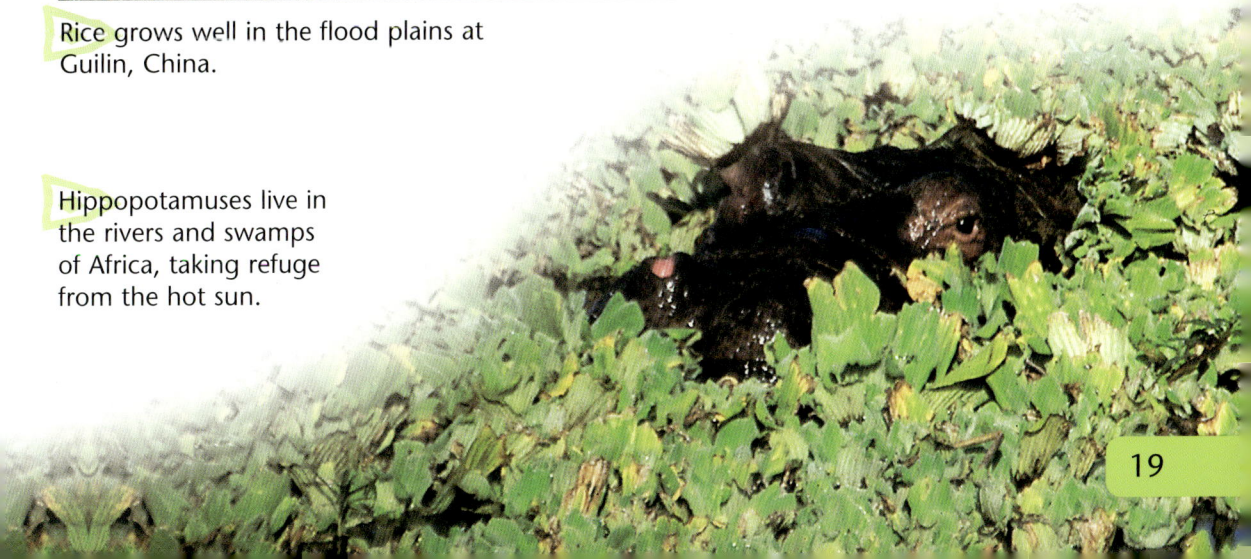

The Yanomami

Several peoples live in the Amazon rainforest. Here, the 27,000 Yanomami (yah-NOH-mom-ee) have kept their traditional way of life. These native peoples of the rainforest are hunters and gatherers as well as farmers. They burn a small patch of jungle to create a field. Many different plants are grown in the field for food and medicine. After a few years, the soil begins to lose its nutrients. Each cleared patch is then given ten to fifty years to rest and regrow while the farmers move on to clear new fields. This type of farming is called **shifting cultivation**.

However, modern restrictions on land use are causing problems for shifting cultivation. The Yanomami are not allowed enough land to allow for proper rest and regrowth. The soil becomes infertile, and the rainforest is permanently damaged and destroyed.

Map showing where the Yanomami people live

A Yanomami man felling trees to clear land for crops

A large Yanomami house (top right) with a newly cleared patch of forest nearby

The Yanomami traditionally depended on hunting and fishing. As more of the rainforest is lost, however, the animals that the Yanomami hunt, such as deer, monkeys and tapirs, are more difficult to find. In 1992, to protect the Yanomami, the Brazilian government set aside about 9.4 million hectares of land as a Yanomami reserve.

A traditional Yanomami home, known as a *yano*

Each Yanomami community lives in a ring-shaped group house called a *yano*. Each family has its own hearth and hammocks for sleeping. The people have no written language. Instead, they use chants and stories to preserve their history. The Yanomami are proud of their culture and believe everything on the land is sacred. They believe that if they use the land around them wisely, the land in turn will take care of them.

A Yanomami family relaxing in its hearth

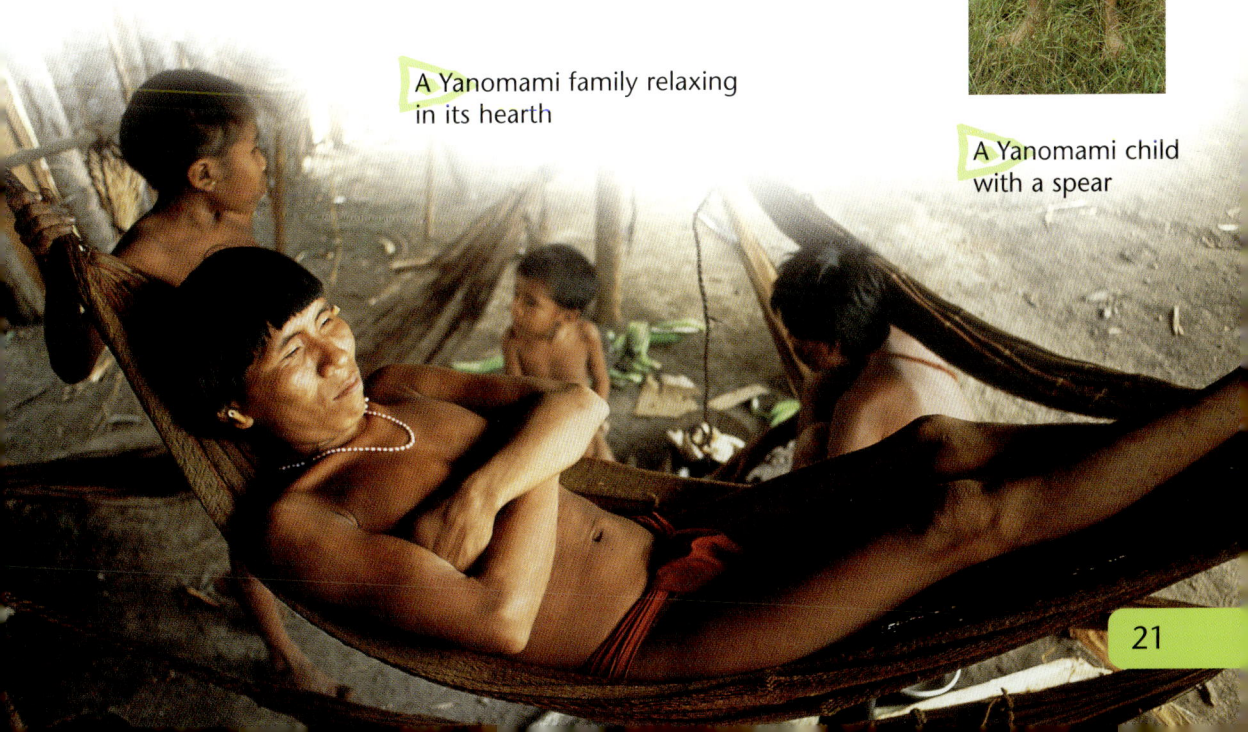
A Yanomami child with a spear

The Seminole

The Seminole (SEM-ihn-ohl) people are a Native American group who live mostly in Florida. In 1819, the United States acquired Florida from Spain and attempted to remove the Seminole from the land. This resulted in years of war. Some Seminole were marched west to Oklahoma and placed on reservations.

Map showing the Everglades region where the Seminole live

However, most managed to stay in Florida. They hid in the Everglades and lived by hunting and fishing. Because they often needed to flee, the Seminole developed houses that could be built and taken down quickly. They found that leaves from palmetto trees, which grew all around, made a good thatch roof over a cypress log frame. They could easily put up these homes on swampy ground or rebuild them after a hurricane.

These Seminole people are thatching the roof of a *chikee,* or house.

Some Florida Seminole continue to live in these houses, and make their living by selling traditional crafts. Seminole use palmetto fibre to make cotton-stuffed dolls in colourfully striped outfits. They sell the dolls, as well as clothing, paintings and grass baskets to tourists.

Brightly coloured Seminole dolls are still made today and are sold to tourists.

Seminole people retain many aspects of their traditional **culture**. At harvest time, for example, they perform the Green Corn Dance. This is a time to settle tribal arguments and mark the coming of age of young people. Because there is no written language, storytelling also remains central to the Seminole heritage.

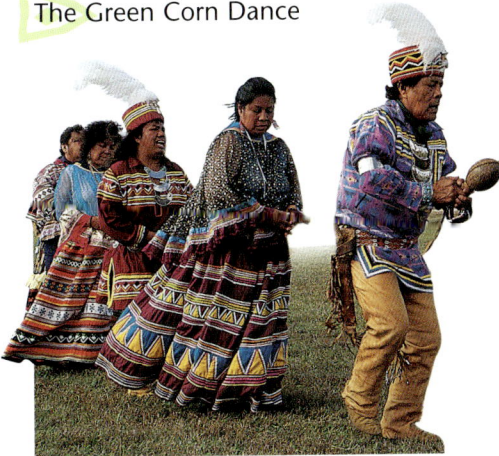
The Green Corn Dance

One of the concerns of the Seminole tribal governement is to keep the Everglades clean and unspoiled. To preserve its environment and identity, the Seminole nation has created a plan to improve water quality and control floods.

The Seminole run tours to teach people about their history and the Everglades environment.

23

The Bangladeshis

Most of Bangladesh (bang-luh-DESH), is formed from the **delta** of two great rivers, the Ganges and the Brahmaputra. From June to October, the **monsoon** season brings heavy rains that flood Bangladesh's rivers and delta land. The silt left behind when the water recedes makes the land fertile for farming. The flooding, however, is dangerous. During the heavy monsoon of 1998, for example, 30 million Bangladeshis lost their homes to floods.

Map showing where the Bangladeshi people live

To avoid flooding, many homes in the delta are built on tall stilts. Boats and rafts carry goods to market. Boats are so important in Bangladesh that boat songs, called *bhatiali*, are one of the most popular types of music.

Many Bangladeshi houses are built on stilts to protect them from floods.

Agriculture in Bangladesh is limited to plants that thrive in a wet environment. Jute, the country's major export, grows well on the **flood plain**. This tough, fibrous plant is used to make burlap (tough fabric) and rope. Rice is the leading food crop, and legumes (beans) are second. Fish, readily available in the rivers, is the chief source of animal protein for most Bangladeshis.

The fibrous plant, jute, is used to make rope.

Life is not easy. Roads and railways are difficult to build and maintain. Bangladesh cannot afford to build bridges, so slow ferry-boats are used to cross most waterways. Flood-control projects are needed to make living and farming in the delta easier.

Bangladeshi children catching fish with nets

Ferries are one of the main forms of transport in Bangladesh and are often very crowded.

25

Life in Mountainous Lands

Strong winds, thin air, cold nights and rugged terrain make mountain life difficult. Mountain animals must be able to keep their balance on steep slopes. They also need thick fur to survive the cold winds.

Plant life varies with the altitude. Deciduous trees – trees that lose their leaves each year – may grow at the foot of a mountain. Higher up, where it is colder, evergreen forests grow. Above the tree line, bogs and meadows appear. Higher still, bare rock is often capped with snow.

Traditionally, mountain peoples herd animals. The goats of the European Alps, the yaks of Asia's Himalayas and the llamas of South America's Andes are a few examples of these animals.

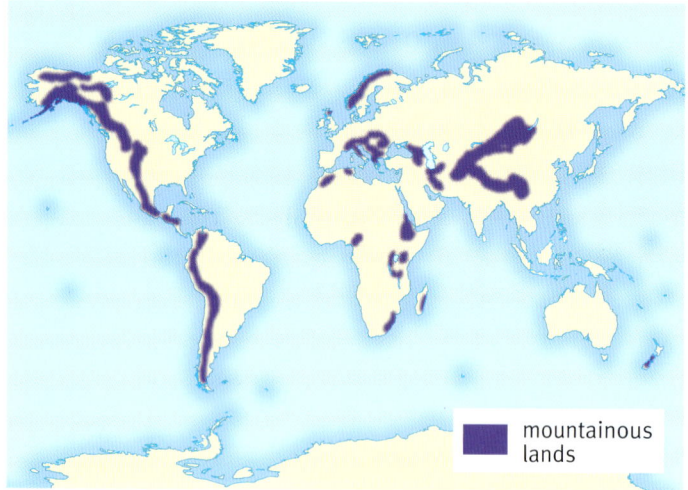

mountainous lands

Map showing the mountainous regions of the world

The agile ibex can scramble over craggy rocks with ease.

The mountainous terrain of the Swiss Alps

The Aymara

The Andes Mountains stretch for 8,000 kilometres down the Pacific coast of South America. This is the longest mountain range in the world. In Bolivia, a high plain called the Altiplano (ahl-tee-PLAH-noh) runs between two chains of the Andes. The Altiplano is cold, dry, windy and almost treeless. However, almost three-quarters of Bolivia's population live there. Many of them are Aymara (eye-mah-RAH) – an ancient people who have always lived in the mountains.

Map showing where the Aymara people live

Aymara farmers plowing in the Altiplano region

Despite the poor land quality and harsh climate, many Aymara farm on the Altiplano. The potato, which is native to South America, grows well on the high plains. Barley and wheat are also important crops.

A family may also raise cows, sheep, pigs, chickens and rabbits. Llamas, native to the Andes, are pack animals used for transport, clothing, fuel and food. In such a harsh climate, the people must know how to put every resource to its utmost use.

Many Aymara have moved from their traditional homes to towns and cities, such as La Paz, Bolivia's capital. Many Aymara like to watch football on television or go into town. Aymara children in village schools usually study both Spanish and the Aymara language and **culture**.

These Aymara girls are wearing wool hats and layers of clothes to protect them from cold winds.

Mountain Music

The music of the Andes is known worldwide. Reed panpipes, called *chuqui*, are often the only instruments in an Aymara village band.

Llamas are used to transport goods.

The Sherpa

The Himalayas are the world's tallest mountains. The Himalayan range stretches 2,500 kilometres from east to west across Asia, mostly in northern India, Nepal and Bhutan. Mount Everest, the world's highest peak, is in the Himalayas.

Map showing where the Sherpa people live

One of the few groups living in this area is the Sherpa of Nepal. Most Sherpas live in small farming villages in houses made of stone and mud, with thatch for roofs. Like the Aymara, Sherpas grow crops that thrive at high altitudes, such as potatoes, barley, wheat and maize (corn). The Sherpa also use yaks, shaggy-haired relatives of oxen, as plough animals. Yaks are a source of milk, meat and leather.

A traditional Sherpa house

Yaks and herders at their camp

These Sherpas are porters for a tourist expedition.

If you were to climb high into the Himalayas, you would probably suffer from mountain sickness. The lack of oxygen in the air would make you dizzy, and you might faint. The Sherpa, however, are used to the thin air. Because of this, many Sherpas become guides and porters for mountain-climbing expeditions. Sherpas are usually included in the groups that climb Mount Everest. In 1953, Sherpa Tenzing Norgay and Sir Edmund Hillary were the first people to reach the top of the world's highest mountain.

Saturday is market day in Namche Bazaar, the main town in the Sherpa region. The town can only be reached on foot.

Conclusion

Throughout the world, people have adapted to harsh climates and terrain. They have made full use of the resources, plants and animals that are available to them. In their struggle to survive, they have shown great ingenuity and creativity.

With the spread of modern civilization, people living in harsh lands continue to adapt. Most have used modern tools to make life easier. Others who have lost their land have found work in the modern economy. Generally, however, traditional customs and activities survive. In this way, the peoples of harsh lands maintain a living link to their past.

Glossary

cultures	ways of life, including beliefs, customs and traditions of particular peoples
delta	a deposit of sand and soil that collects at the mouth of a river
deserts	dry regions, usually receiving less than 25 centimetres of rain a year
flood plain	land that is periodically flooded by a river
indigenous	native to or first in an area
monsoon	winds in southern Asia that bring months of heavy rain
nomads	people who move from place to place
permafrost	frozen soil
savannahs	grasslands with few or no trees
semi-deserts	dry regions that receive about 38 centimetres of rainfall a year
shifting cultivation	a farming method in which forest land is cleared and planted for a few years and then left fallow as the farmers move to new fields
swamps	lowlands that are covered with slow-moving water
tropical rainforests	thick forests in the warm regions around the equator that receive frequent heavy rain
tundra	the treeless land surrounding the Arctic Ocean at the northern edges of Europe, Asia and North America